D1542092

ALL ABOUT...

THE

Industrial Revolution

PETER HEPPLEWHITE
AND
MAIRI CAMPBELL

Printed in 2015
Copyright © Wayland 2015
Text © Peter Hepplewhite and Mairi Campbell 2015
Illustrations © Dez Marwood 2015
All rights reserved.

ISBN: 9780750294850
10 9 8 7 6 5 4 3 2 1

First published in Great Britain in 2002 by Wayland

Wayland, an imprint of Hachette Children's Group
Part of Hodder & Stoughton
Carmelite House, 50 Victoria Embankment
London EC4Y 0DZ

An Hachette UK Company
www.hachette.co.uk
www.hachettechildrens.co.uk

Printed in China

Editor: Liz Gorgerly
Inside design: Mark Whitechurch
Maps and graphs: Peter Bull
Picture credits: cover. Shutterstock: Lipskiy, Vitaly Korovin, LiliGraphie, Perfect Gui. The Beamish Museum – 37. Private Collection – 9b, 13t, 13b, 29t, 41. Royal Academy of Arts – 31. Leeds Museums and Galleries – 35b. V&A Museum – 38. Mary Evans – 8, 26t, 26b, 27, 28, 33, 35t, 36b, 39b. © Norfolk Museums Service – 42b. Peter Newark – 14, 23b, 24. Science and Society Picture Library – 6, 7, 9t, 10t, 10b, 12, 15t, 15b, 16, 17t, 17b, 18t, 18b, 20b, 22, 23t, 25.

THE

Industrial Revolution

PETER HEPPLEWHITE
AND
MAIRI CAMPBELL

Wayland

an imprint of Hodder Children's Books

TIMELINE

1709 *Abraham Darby I buys the Coalbrookdale works. He discovers coke can be used to smelt iron.*

1712 *Thomas Newcomen develops steam-powered pump.*

1761 *Opening of the Bridgewater Canal, one of the first in Britain.*

1765 *Hargreaves invents spinning jenny for spinning thread.*

1787 *Cartwright invents power-loom for weaving cloth.*

1788 *James Watt improves the steam engine.*

1801 *First census is taken.*

1812 *Luddites attack machines in cities of northern England.*

1815 *Sir Humphrey Davy and George Stephenson both invent safety lamps for miners.*

1825 Locomotion No. 1 *runs on the Stockton to Darlington Railway.*

1829 *Stephenson's* Rocket *wins the Rainhill Trials.*

1831 *Cholera epidemic starts in Sunderland.*

1833 *Factory Act stops children working until they are nine years old.*

1834 *Tolpuddle Martyrs transported to Australia.*

1834 *Poor Law Amendment Act sets up workhouses.*

1837 *First telegraph message is sent.*

1839 *James Nasmyth invents the steam hammer for shaping iron.*

1840 *Cheap postal service is introduced.*

1842 *Mines Act bans women and children from working underground.*

1851 *The Great Exhibition is held in London.*

1851 *Census shows that more people are living in towns than in the country.*

1852 *Palmer's shipyard launches the* John Bowes.

1856 *Henry Bessemer's converter halves the cost of steel production.*

1866 *Football Association is set up.*

1870 *Forster's Education Act is passed.*

1876 *Alexander Graham Bell invents the telephone.*

1987 *Ironbridge Gorge is designated a World Heritage Site.*

CONTENTS

THE FIRST INDUSTRIAL NATION

Have you ever played a computer game, ridden in a car or gone on holiday in a jumbo jet? These are all products of the hi-tech age we live in – an age that began over 250 years ago with the start of the Industrial Revolution. Revolution means a complete change – turning things upside down. Industrial means using machines.

The Darby iron works at Coalbrookdale. They have been called the cradle of the Industrial Revolution by historians because the remarkable Darby family discovered how to make cheap iron (see page 16).

George Stephenson's Locomotion No. 1 *carrying the first passengers along the Stockton to Darlington railway on September 27 1825. This was the first passenger railway in the world.*

In 1700 most people lived and worked in the countryside. Over the next 150 years, this traditional lifestyle was turned upside down by a wave of new ideas and inventions. Factories were built and people flocked into the towns to find work. Canals and railways were constructed to move raw materials to the factories and to take finished goods to market. By 1850 the British confidently called their country the workshop of the world.

7

THE DOMESTIC SYSTEM

Before the Industrial Revolution craftsmen and their families worked at home or in small workshops. All types of goods were made by hand including nails, lace, stockings, shoes and textiles. Historians call this the domestic system.

In Yorkshire, where a lot of woollen cloth was made, merchants bought raw wool and took it to outworkers to make cloth. Whole families worked together.

Women working at home spinning flax for linen on spinning wheels. Can you see the boy by the fire and the family pets?

Children could wash and card (comb) the wool for their mothers to spin into yarn. Finally, the yarn was woven into cloth by their fathers on hand-powered looms.

Many families also had a small plot of land to grow vegetables and keep hens, a goat or cow. It took them long hours to make money but they could choose when they wanted to work.

The woven yarn would be taken to a workshop to be 'finished'. This made it thicker and ready to use.

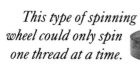

This type of spinning wheel could only spin one thread at a time.

The First Factories

New machines were invented that could spin many threads at once, such as James Hargreaves's spinning jenny (1765), Richard Arkwright's water frame (1769) and Samuel Crompton's spinning mule (1779). These were powered by large water-wheels, which meant they could not be used at home. Factories, where one large water-wheel could power all the equipment, steadily took over from the domestic system.

Hargreaves's spinning jenny. The first machines could only spin 8 threads but were soon improved to spin 100 threads. Jenny meant machine.

Richard Arkwright was a successful mill owner and inventor. His water frame was bought by mill owners all over Britain.

Women and girls use carding engines to comb wool in Swainson Birley Mill in Preston, 1834.

The speed of the new spinning machines meant that weavers using hand-looms could not keep up. In 1787 Edmund Cartwright invented a power-loom. By 1829 there were 49,000 power-looms in mills all over Britain. One worker could operate four looms at a time, making them cheap to run. In the new factories the workers had to follow the strict rules laid down by their bosses such as not going to the toilet without asking permission.

POWER – WATER AND STEAM

Before 1700, industry was run by human and animal power, or from nature – wind and water. As the demand for energy soared, the most important power resource became water.

You can visit this huge water-wheel at Laxey on the Isle of Man. It was built in 1854, measures 22 metres across, and was used to pump water from a lead mine. The wheel could lift 1,000 litres of water from a depth of 300 metres every minute.

Giant water-wheels could drive whole factories of machines. Better still, once the wheel was built, the power was free. But water-wheels were dependent upon perfect weather conditions – low rainfall and drought in summer, or ice in winter, could stop them turning.

In 1712 Thomas Newcomen built an engine for raising water by fire – a steam engine. It was large, clumsy and expensive to run, but it was not affected by the weather.

Steam power was a vital breakthrough. Steam engines could be built anywhere, not just by fast-flowing streams. By 1800 there were around 1,250 steam engines running in Britain. Even so, it was not until the 1850s that steam power took over from water power.

A steam engine designed by Scottish engineer James Watt. He didn't invent the steam engine but he did improve the design.

COAL MINING

With the invention of the steam engine, demand for coal rocketed. In 1700 about 2.54 million tonnes of coal were mined in Britain, by 1900 this had risen to 224 million tonnes.

Deaths in Coal Mines

Cause of Death	1838	1864
Explosion of fire-damp	80	94
Roof collapses	97	395
Falls of items down shafts	4	51
Fell down shaft	66	64
Drowning	22	11
By wagons	21	56

A coal mine in about 1800. The smoke comes from the steam engine that powered the pump. Deep mines needed to be drained or they would have flooded.

Many coal mines suffered disasters when flames from lamps caused a gas called fire-damp to explode. Safety lamps like these saved thousands of lives by stopping the fire-damp from reaching the flame.

As coal near the surface was used up, mines became deeper and more dangerous for the miners. The coal was cut by hand with a pick-axe. Sometimes miners worked in seams no higher than 75 centimetres. Children as young as five years old worked as 'trappers' – opening and closing airtight trap doors to make sure fresh air circulated round the mine. Women and girls carried baskets of coal as heavy as 150 kilos on their backs, often wading through water up to their knees.

Hauling baskets of coal from the bottom of the shaft to the surface. Some of the miners are women.

15

IRON AND STEEL

In 1700 the iron industry was in decline. Ironworkers needed charcoal to smelt the iron ore in their furnaces. But charcoal was in short supply, because the wood needed to make it was expensive.

During the eighteenth century three generations of the remarkable Darby family solved this problem. Abraham Darby I (1677–1717) bought the Coalbrookdale works on the River Severn in 1709.

The Ironbridge was opened in 1779. It was the first large bridge in the world to be built from iron and has become the symbol of the Industrial Revolution throughout the world.

Making plough shares for farmers at the Britannia Iron Works in Bedford.

Iron Production	
1750	30.480 t
1800	254.000 t
1850	2.03 million t
1900	9.14 million t

He discovered that iron could be made with coke instead of charcoal. His son, Abraham Darby II (1711–63), found out how to make better coke by burning coal in ovens. This coke made better quality iron. His grandson, Abraham Darby III (1750–91), built the famous iron bridge over the Severn Gorge near Coalbrookdale. This became a tourist attraction and showed people that almost anything could be made from iron. By 1850 Britain made over 2 million tonnes of iron – half the world's supply.

Steel was stronger and less brittle than iron but difficult to make until Henry Bessemer invented his converter in 1856. This turned molten iron into steel in 20 minutes.

James Nasmyth invented the steam hammer in 1839. It was used to shape large iron objects, like propeller shafts for ships, quickly and carefully.

RAILWAYS AND CANALS

In 1700 the best way to move heavy goods like cotton or coal around Britain was by sea or river. But many areas were difficult to reach other than by cart or packhorse. One solution was to build man-made rivers

called canals. By 1825, 1,500 kilometres of canal had been constructed by armies of labourers called navvies.

George Stephenson's Rocket *won the Rainhill Trials in 1829, a competition to find the best locomotive for the new Liverpool to Manchester railway. This was the first inter-city service.*

The Bridgewater Canal was one of the first to be built in Britain. Opened in 1761, it ran 12 kilometres between Worsley and Manchester. A passing traveller called it 'a canal in the air'. Can you see the narrowboats, the canal barges, being towed across?

Yet by 1850 the haulage trade, moving heavy goods, had been snatched from canals by another form of transport – the railway. Steam-driven locomotives that travelled along tracks were quicker and cheaper. Father and son George and Robert Stephenson were amongst the greatest railway engineers of the day. By 1870 24,000 kilometres of railway track had been laid.

The Britannia Bridge, over the Menai Strait in Wales, was designed by Robert Stephenson and opened in 1850. It was a stunning new idea – the trains would travel through a bridge made out of two long iron tubes.

SHIPBUILDING

Brunel at the launch of his third ship, the Great Eastern, *in 1858. At 207 metres long she was the biggest in the world – and remained so for the next 40 years.*

I n the eighteenth century ships were still made of wood and powered by sails. Most people thought iron ships would fall apart in a storm or steam engines break down on a long voyage. One man set out to prove them wrong – the brilliant engineer Isambard Kingdom Brunel.

The Royal Navy launched its first iron hulled battleship – HMS Warrior in 1860. After this all the navy's warships were built of iron.

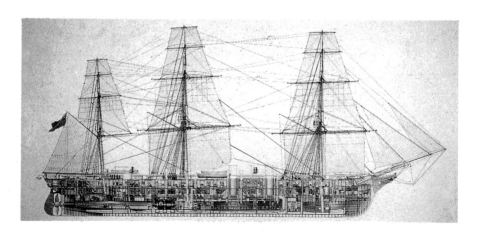

The first ship designed by Brunel was the *Great Western* – a wooden vessel with a steam engine driving paddle wheels. His second ship, the *Great Britain*, was made of iron and powered by a propeller. Using these ideas, Palmer's shipyard in Jarrow launched the first modern cargo ship, the *John Bowes* in 1852. She had an iron hull, steam engines and a propeller.

In 1838 the Great Western *just lost the race to be the first steam ship to cross the Atlantic – arriving only hours behind her rival, the* Sirius. *But did the* Sirius *cheat? She had run out of coal and started to burn her cargo, while the* Great Western *had plenty of fuel left.*

COMMUNICATIONS

With industry and towns booming there was a need for better communications. The first newspapers were published weekly and most towns had their own local paper by the late 1700s but they were expensive. Cuts in taxes, cheap paper and steam printing presses meant almost everyone could afford to buy a daily paper by the 1880s.

The Victorians were the first to create a 'World Wide Web'– it was called the telegraph. The first telegraph message was sent in 1837, and in 1840 Samuel Morse invented Morse Code to send quick messages along the wires. In 1866 a telegraph cable was laid under the Atlantic to Canada so that telegrams could be sent between Europe and North America for the first time.

Alexander Graham Bell invented the telephone in 1876. Words were turned into electrical impulses, sent along a wire and turned back into speech.

THE TELEGRAPH.

Many telegraph operators were women, as the cover of this song sheet shows.

GEORGE LEYBOURNE.

In 1840 Rowland Hill set up the Post Office as we know it and introduced cheap stamps. One old penny stamp (worth about 0.5p today) paid for a letter no matter how far it was going.

A Penny Black stamp with the head of Queen Victoria.

National newspapers like the Daily Telegraph *brought news from all over the world into Victorian homes. Can you find out what happened at Mafeking?*

23

THE GREAT EXHIBITION

The Great Exhibition was organized by Prince Albert, the husband of Queen Victoria, to celebrate British industry. It was held in the Crystal Palace, Hyde Park, London and opened on 1 May 1851.

Over six million people visited the Exhibition, coming from all over the country by train. The first travel agent Thomas Cook sold 165,000 excursion tickets.

The Crystal Palace was a brilliant design by Joseph Paxton. It was a prefabricated building of iron and glass made in factories and put together on site, like a giant greenhouse. This picture shows the Crystal Palace after it was moved to Sydenham in 1852.

Some days the admission fee was £1, on others 1 shilling (about 5p today). Everyone could afford to go but the upper classes could have the expensive days to themselves. Queen Victoria visited and wrote in her diary: 'We remained two hours and a half and I came back quite beaten and my head bewildered from the myriads of beautiful and wonderful things.'

There were 19,000 exhibits inside the Crystal Palace including a huge Nasmyth steam hammer (see page 17) and the giant hydraulic pumps which had lifted the tubes of the Britannia Railway Bridge into place (see page 19). This picture shows the transept, the main aisle with a domed roof.

WORKING CONDITIONS AND THE FIRST REFORMS

Mills were hot, noisy and crowded places to work. Men, women and children toiled for at least 12 hours a day, six days a week, for low wages. Mill owners liked to employ women and children – they could pay them less than men. There were very strict rules – workers could be fined for whistling, being late or having dirty hands.

Children being winched down a mineshaft in Yorkshire. The Earl of Shaftesbury came to the aid of children in the mines with the 1842 Mines Act. This banned boys under the age of ten, girls and women from working underground.

Here you can see mill workers surrounded by power-looms. The mill was kept warm and damp so that the cotton threads stayed strong. Many of the workers became ill with lung diseases.

Young children called 'piecers' crawled underneath moving machinery to mend broken threads. This was dangerous and there were often accidents. People were shocked that children had to work so hard and laws were passed to try and make things better.

Anthony Ashley, the 7th Earl of Shaftesbury, was a devout Christian who thought it was wrong for children to be badly treated. He campaigned for new laws to help them.

The 7th Earl of Shaftesbury was responsible for the 1833 Factory Act which stopped children working until they were nine years old. Children aged nine to thirteen could only work eight hours a day and then had to go to school for two hours.

THE LUDDITES ATTACK

The machines of the Industrial Revolution made profits for the factory owners but took away the livelihoods of others. Skilled textile workers, like hand-loom weavers, were thrown out of work or had their wages cut when steam-powered looms were brought in.

From 1812 to 1814 groups of workers across Lancashire, Nottinghamshire and Yorkshire attacked factories. They burned or smashed the machines that had driven them to the edge of starvation. Bosses were threatened and even murdered. Rumours spread that the rioters were led by a mysterious leader – Ned Ludd or King Ludd.

A cartoon of a machine-wrecker disguised as a woman. He is urging his companions to attack another factory.

In a letter to a mill owner in Huddersfield Ned Ludd wrote: 'Information has been given that you are the holder of those detestable shearing frames. I shall send one of my lieutenants with at least 300 men to destroy them and burn your building to ashes …'

Troops were called in and the Luddites were scared off or arrested. Seventeen machine-breakers were executed at York in 1812 and others transported to Australia.

A cartoon of a mob of Luddites. Can you tell what the artist thinks of the mob from this picture?

A poster offers a reward of £200 for information leading to the arrest of Luddites in Stockport.

£200. Reward

WHEREAS

The *WAREHOUSE of Mr. William Radcliffe*, COTTON MANUFACTURER, ADJOINING TO HIS DWELLING-HOUSE IN THE HIGHER HILLGATE, STOCKPORT, IN THE COUNTY OF CHESTER,

Was, between the Hours of **2** and **3** in the Morning of **FRIDAY** the **20**th of March, instant,

Wilfully, maliciously, & feloniously

Set on Fire,

By some wicked and desperate Incendiaries, who broke the Windows thereof, and threw in five Flambeaux or Torches, composed of Pitch, Tar, Oakum, and Spirits of Turpentine; and some Waste Cops of Cotton-weft, which had been dipped in similar Spirits.

The Villains left on the Outside of the said Warehouse, three Clubs or large Sticks of a peculiar Sort, which may be the future Means of a Discovery.

A Reward of **£200.** will be paid to the Person who may give such Information as may lead to the Discovery and Conviction of the Principals concerned in this diabolical Crime, upon Application to

J. LLOYD, *Solicitor.*

Stockport, March **21**st, **1812.**

LOMAX, PRINTER.

TRADES UNIONS

Some workers realized that the only way to improve their wages and working conditions was to join together by forming trades unions. Unions collected funds to help members in hard times, such as sickness or injury, and bargained with their bosses.

A procession by dock workers during a strike in 1889.

Early unions worried the government so much that they were banned from 1799 to 1824. Yet even when they were legal, members faced persecution. Five farm labourers in Dorset who tried to set up a trades union were arrested for swearing an illegal oath on the Bible. They were transported to Australia in 1834.

Skilled craftsmen, like engineers and carpenters, had more success in forming New Model Trades Unions in the 1850s. They earned high wages, so could afford high membership fees and pay full-time union officials to bargain with employers.

The decision to strike wasn't an easy one. Families often used all their savings and went hungry. Sometimes people were evicted from their homes.

MAKING SENSE OF THE CENSUS

I n the 1700s no one knew how many people lived in Britain. And this was a worry! The government needed the figures to answer some important questions:

- Was the number of people growing or falling?
- How many people worked on farms and how many people worked in industry?
- How many men could serve in the army and navy?

The only way to find out was to count all the people. This official count of the population would be called the census.

The census return for a Newcastle family in 1881. The information includes names, addresses, ages and jobs. You can find out about the Victorians who lived near you by looking at the census returns in your local library.

At census time, every family was visited by an enumerator. He handed out and collected in the census forms. If no one could write, the enumerator helped to fill in the form.

In 1801 the first census was taken and it was discovered that the population of England and Wales was 8,892,536, with another 1,608,420 in Scotland – a total of 10.5 million people.

From this time, the census was held every ten years. In 1851 the census recorded an historic change. The population of Britain had soared to nearly 21 million (20,816,351). And, for the first time, over half of them lived in towns and cities, not the countryside.

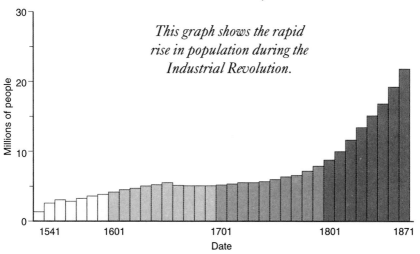

This graph shows the rapid rise in population during the Industrial Revolution.

TOWNS, CITIES AND OVERCROWDING

When people wanted to visit a modern industrial town they went to places like Manchester or Leeds. And many didn't like what they saw! Workers lived close by their factories in terraces of small houses. These were built quickly, and often poorly, to give homes to the people who were moving in to find work.

Slums like these were grim places to live. Most had no drains or running water and were often damp and cold. Wages were not high enough to pay the rent for a whole house so families often lived crammed into one room. Toilets were in huts in the yard and were shared by

several houses. The streets were not paved and were full of rubbish. Factory chimneys belched out filthy smoke polluting the atmosphere and blocking out the light.

Slum-dwellers. Their homes were very close together. There were no gardens or places to play.

Better-off people moved away from the dirty factories to suburbs, where they built large houses with gardens. Many of these richer families had servants: maids, a cook and a gardener.

Population Table

City	1801	1851	1871
Glasgow	77,000	345,000	522,000
Newcastle	33,000	88,000	128,000
Manchester	75,000	303,000	351,000
London	959,000	2,362,000	3,254,000

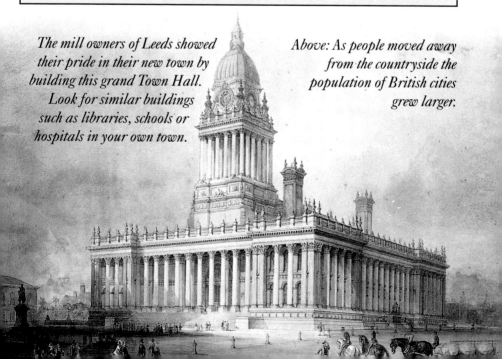

The mill owners of Leeds showed their pride in their new town by building this grand Town Hall. Look for similar buildings such as libraries, schools or hospitals in your own town.

Above: As people moved away from the countryside the population of British cities grew larger.

DIRT, DEATH AND DISEASE

Overcrowded slums were not only dirty places, they were dangerous. Hundreds of people crammed together meant that diseases such as tuberculosis, typhoid and cholera could spread easily. In Manchester in the 1840s, 57 out of every 100 children died before they were five years old.

This cartoon pokes fun at the new idea of germs by showing imaginary monsters hiding in a drop of London water.

Florence Nightingale (1820-1910) ran a hospital for injured soldiers at Scutari during the Crimean War. Later she worked hard to make nursing a well-trained and highly regarded job.

There were two cholera epidemics in 1831 and 1849, which killed thousands. The government started to look at how to improve the health of the people. Public Health Acts were passed which meant that towns had to provide clean drinking water, build sewers and arrange to have rubbish collected.

Scientists made important discoveries in medicine. The French scientist Louis Pasteur proved that disease was caused by germs or bacteria, not by bad smells as once believed. Vaccination against diseases such as smallpox and diphtheria was introduced. The Scottish doctor Joseph Lister found that antiseptic could be used to prevent the spread of infection.

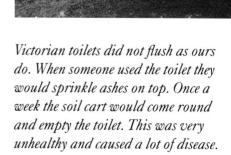

Victorian toilets did not flush as ours do. When someone used the toilet they would sprinkle ashes on top. Once a week the soil cart would come round and empty the toilet. This was very unhealthy and caused a lot of disease.

THE POOR

From 1599 every parish had to collect rates to pay for the poor in the area. The very young, old or sick were cared for in the workhouse. Those who were able to look after themselves were given money or food to help them live in their own homes.

Between 1775 and 1832 the cost of looking after the poor soared from £1.5 million to £7 million. This caused a great debate in Parliament. Some people argued that the old ways of looking after the poor encouraged idleness and large families.

A Shoe Black boy working in a Victorian street. Many large towns had a Shoe Black Brigade, a charity to train poor and homeless boys to shine shoes for a living and keep them out of the workhouse.

The dining hall in a large workhouse. Food was basic and not very appetizing.

In 1834 the government passed the Poor Law Amendment Act – a stricter and cheaper way of dealing with poverty. Now everyone wanting help, such as the unemployed, old or sick people, had to go into a workhouse. Families were split up while paupers had to wear uniforms and have their hair cut short to stop the spread of lice. Men did unpleasant jobs like crushing bones to make glue while the women cleaned the workhouse and made the meals. Poor people who did not obey the rules were punished by putting them on a diet of bread and water.

Dr Thomas John Barnardo founded more than 90 homes for destitute children. The first, in the East End of London, opened in 1870.

EDUCATION

Until the late 1900s most parents had to pay to send their children to school. Wealthy families sent their sons to public schools like Eton or Harrow where they learnt Greek and Latin. Their daughters stayed at home with a governess and learnt to draw, sing and play the piano.

The first schools for the poor were run by religious groups, such as the Society for the Propagation of Christian Knowledge formed in 1699. The pupils were taught reading, writing and Bible stories. Other children went to Dame Schools, run by old ladies in their own homes.

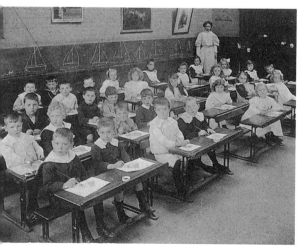

They were looked after but didn't learn much at all. There were no free schools, parents had to find at least one penny per child each week.

These children are having a drawing lesson. They didn't have all the colourful art materials you can use.

In this Ragged School all the children are crammed in one room. In spite of the conditions many children gained a basic education and found jobs.

The 7th Earl of Shaftesbury founded the Ragged School Union in 1844 to set up schools in the slum areas of the new towns. Pupils were taught the 3 Rs – Reading, wRiting and aRithmetic – so they could find jobs and stay away from crime.

In 1870 Forster's Education Act meant that the government would build and run schools if local charity schools did not provide enough places. It wasn't until the 1880 Education Act that compulsory education began – all children between five and ten years old had to go to school, whether their parents wanted them to or not.

LEISURE FOR EVERYONE

At first, ordinary people in the new industrial towns spent most days working. What little spare time they had was used to drink, gamble or watch cruel sports like bull-baiting and cock-fighting. And they had to be careful – a soldier was gored to death when he stood too close to a bull-bait in Newcastle in 1768.

Boys toss a cricket bat to see who will bat first. Cricket was already a popular game by 1800.

The Industrial Revolution affected toys too. Cheap, factory-made toys brought new excitement to children's lives.

By the end of the nineteenth century people had more free time and many of the sports we enjoy today had become popular such as football, cricket, golf, rugby and tennis. The Football Association was set up in 1866 and the Football League in 1888. The first visit by an Australian cricket team came in 1878 – the beginning of a rivalry that still goes on today.

Cheap train fares made day-trips to the coast possible for millions of working people. Seaside resorts boomed and parks, piers and promenades were built. Other popular pastimes included visits to the circus and music hall. In the age before radio and TV many homes had a piano and a collection of song sheets.

A day out at the seaside. By 1900 over half the population of the country went to the seaside at least once a year.

VISITING THE INDUSTRIAL REVOLUTION

O ne of the most exciting ways to learn about the Industrial Revolution is to see it for yourself. You can ride on a tram at the Beamish museum, go down a mine in the Black Country Museum or stand on the deck of Brunel's wonderful *Great Britain* in Bristol docks.

This map shows you only a few of the large industrial attractions. To find out what sites are near you contact your local tourist information service.

Scottish Mining Museum (**Newtongrange**)

Scottish Maritime Museum (**Irvine**)

Beamish North of England Open Air Museum (**Beamish**)

National Railway Museum (**York**)

Museum of Science and Industry (**Manchester**)

National Tramway Museum (**Matlock**)

Merseyside Maritime Museum (**Liverpool**)

Sir Richard Arkwright's Cromford Mill (**Cromford**)

Ironbridge Gorge Museums Trust (**Ironbridge**)

Black Country Living Museum (**Dudley**)

National Waterways Museum (**Gloucester**)

Big Pit Mining Museum (**Blaenafon**)

Science Museum (**London**)

Ragged School Museum (**London**)

SS Great Britain (**Bristol**)

Cornish Mines and Engines & Cornwall Industrial Discovery Centre (**Pool**)

Today spectacular sites like these are still sources of great pride, helping local communities by attracting thousands of tourists. Some, like the museums of the Ironbridge Gorge, in Shropshire, are so famous that they have been selected as a World Heritage Site by UNESCO (United Nations Educational, Scientific and Cultural Organization).

Most museums and historic sites have free promotional leaflets. You can make your own souvenir collection of places you've visited.

GLOSSARY

antiseptic *A disinfectant that kills germs.*

bacteria *Tiny living things or organisms which can cause disease.*

bull-baiting *A cruel sport in which ferocious dogs are set on bulls. The audience bets on the animal they think will kill the other.*

campaign *To take action to change an injustice. This might involve making demonstrations, talking to journalists and writing to Members of Parliament.*

card *A spiky board that is used to comb wool to untangle it ready for spinning.*

coke *Coal which has been burned to remove the impurities so that it can be used to make iron.*

destitute *Poor and homeless.*

enumerator *The person who distributes and collects in census forms.*

epidemic *A serious outbreak of a disease.*

excursion *A cheap one-day trip or holiday.*

hand-loom *A small hand-operated machine which weaves thread or yarn into fabric.*

Morse Code *A code of long and short signals, or dots and dashes, for every letter of the alphabet. Invented by Samuel F. B. Morse, it was used in radio telegraphy.*

pauper *A poor person who is forced to live off charity – a beggar.*

power-loom *A large water or steam-powered machine which weaves thread or yarn into fabric.*

public school *A school that is privately run and charges fees to pupils who study there.*

rates *A tax on property owners.*

rivalry *When a person or group of people compete against each other for the same objective.*

slums *Dirty overcrowded places where poor people live.*

smelt *To heat iron ore and limestone in a blast furnace to separate the iron from the rock.*

suburbs *The area of housing which has been built on the edge of a town where there is more space.*

telegraph *Electric signalling system invented by William Cooke and Charles Wheatstone in 1837.*

transport *To send criminals abroad to serve a prison sentence.*

vaccination *The injection of a mild form of a disease to give protection against that disease.*

INDEX